RISING TOGETHER
LIVING THROUGH A PANDEMIC

ROBERT EDWARDS

Rising Together
Living Through A Pandemic

Copyright © 2021 by Robert Edwards.

Paperback ISBN: 978-1-63812-113-8
Ebook ISBN: 978-1-63812-114-5

All rights reserved. No part in this book may be produced and transmitted in any form or by any means, electronic, or mechanical, including photocopying, recording, or by any information storage and retrieval system, without permission in writing from the copyright owner.

The views expressed in this work are solely those of the author and do not necessarily reflect the views of the publisher hereby disclaims any responsibility for them.

Published by Pen Culture Solutions   09/01/2021

Pen Culture Solutions
1-888-727-7204 (USA)
1-800-950-458 (Australia)
support@penculturesolutions.com

CONTENTS

Dedication vii
Acknowledgements.. 1
Preface 3

The Now Time 6
Image of Self 9
Blink of an Eye 13
Youth 14
Wise Man 15
Magical Smile 17
This New Eden 18
Great Appreciation 19
DNA Show 27
Reasonable Sense 30
The Nature of Love 31
Heart and Soul 37
The Power of Suggestion 41
The Lonesome Gambler 43
Destiny of Pain 47
Life of Pain 51
Life 54
Time 55
Death 56
Soul 57
Faith 58
The obvious is not always right 59
Rising Together 61
Mother and Father 64
Forevermore 67

DEDICATION

I dedicate this collection of poems to the world during the coronavirus Pandemic" And to honor my Father Peter Roy Edwards who died so suddenly.

ACKNOWLEDGEMENTS

I thank my wife, Val, for her support and helping me make time to put my poetry together in this collection. (Words aren't enough to express my gratitude, Val!) Analeise, my daughter, has been truly encouraging and my grandson, Marley, helped inspire me. My sincere thanks to Carl Allport for his greatly talented pictures, and to Richard Treadgold for his astute proofreading. Last but not least a heart-warming thanks to my Mother Patsy and to my Friends for showing loads of faith in me.

PREFACE

I have known Robert Edwards for a number of years. He has an amazing sporting career representing New Zealand at the highest National level in Touch Football. Robert also became a double international sports player when he made selection for the National Samoan 7s Touch World cup side in 1997. Robert has a great passion for writing and Performing Poetry. I recommend Robert's debut book Rising Together, It is a true reflection of his inspiring character and shares with everyone some story telling of his personal thoughts and experiences.

Eddie Dunn, (School Teacher and New Zealand Rugby All Black)

[Edward James Dunn.]
Eddie Dunn

THE NOW TIME

Each and every moment,
With its uncertainty and surprise,
Is equally important
As a century's distant stride.
The ever-present second
Becomes radiant before our eyes;
We should capture and use time now,
For into the past time dies.

The secret to living life
Is to apply the eternal rule,
As we awake each morning with nature
Feeling fresh, crisp and cool,
It's to gain a sense of oneness
And appreciation of all,
Using time as our guide; for example,
To express our unfaltering will.

This experience we live to name,
Let's call it a lifetime,
Is full of learning and growing.
Don't get me wrong,
Can be such a gruelling time,
With joy and sorrow,
Heartache and pain,
Misery and sadness,
Suffering and blame.
But it's just nature's way
Of being cruel to be kind,
All designed for harmony
And peace of mind.

Who weaves time's golden thread?
With endless heavenly cotton
That paved its way through history,
All time now and forgotten,
From when that first stitch was sown (By whom remains unknown)
It still continues to be
Life's ruler of time,
Elegantly measured by the one
Who sits on the throne.

Time gives us opportunity
To lay our mark
Wear our crown.
Time provides us with the chance to say
Before and then, here and now,
Time declares yesterday becomes
Then and thine,
Time suggests tomorrow
Will soon be mine.

Time is the world's director of first and last.
However time's ultimate secret
Lies not in the future or the past.
It is to live each and every moment
In the awesome now-time, so grasp,
Capture time now;
Time changes so fast.

IMAGE OF SELF

Alone in this world I stand
Thinking about myself,
Searching and contemplating
To gain a sense of reality
And a feeling of good health.

Enlightened with clear vision,
It leads me to discover
And just dawns on me
How lucky I am,
With so much untapped wealth.

A forming picture, a conclusion of sorts
Was taking place
In my heart and mind.
A realization, a knowing feeling,
That I wasn't just another
Prisoner to life.

So many opportunities
Presented to me endlessly
And a welcome friend called fate
Was there for me to take.
It was mine, all mine,
If only I believed.

But at times in my life
Self-image takes on ugly shapes.
Its colour pale and flooded,
Its vision blind and fake.

A sense of fear,
A lack of boldness,

A closing grip:
Sometimes I want to give up.
But I can't make that fateful mistake,
If ever in life I feel confused badly,
I just close my eyes
And believe in me.

I make special time to focus on myself,
Defining me each and every day.
I live in the positive,
Not in doubt.
I visualize myself that way.

I apply good values,
I search from within,
I set and achieve my goals;
I go for gold;
I push myself hard,
Right out there on a limb!

Once your image of self
Becomes who you really are,
It's time to be congratulated:
A slightly boastful and bright shining star
Will stand you out wherever you are.
It will be of no surprise.
What a magnificent
Self-image
You have created.

BLINK OF AN EYE

When you think life is hard and you're feeling down
And friends seem to turn a blind eye,
Just consider all those worse off than you—
Show courage and give life a try.

For it's not the problems thrown your way
Nor position in life that counts,
It's to dissolve your tensions, resolve your issues,
Then you are doing quite well.

You see life is short, just a blink of an eye
One moment you're born, the next you die.
So use time wisely and you will survive
Then you'll find things are going just fine.

Enjoy the challenge, have a great time,
But most of all:
Find your spirit . . .
Let it teach you to fly.

YOUTH

When I was a child, wild and young,
Full of energy, dreams and fun,
Enchanted was I, not a care in the world,
Destiny my oyster, my gem, my pearl.

I was so strong, fit and able,
Growing in stature, physically stable.
Little responsibility bound me down
Free as a bird untied from the ground.

Falling in love, starting a family of my own,
The comfort of company, never living alone.
On our land each day protects us well,
Life is great; can't you tell?

Fulfilling my visions, achieving my goals
So much to do before I grow old
Happiness and success all the way through.
My mission, my duty, my dreams came true.

WISE MAN

A young man lived to succeed; he strived
To accumulate possessions whilst he was alive;
Make his fortune; get his own way in life.
My question to you: was this man wise?

Wealth he did take that the world had to offer
Disregarding the needy for him not to bother,
Ignoring with intention the struggling who fall
My question to you: was he wise at all?

Take the old man who has nothing but his smile.
In your moment of need appears his hand for a while.
He craves not for possessions or material wealth,
Rather helping fellow man before himself.

This was the young man with his selfish life;
His journey through time changed his insight.
He realized in giving inner rewards were high.
My answer to you: that young man got wise!

MAGICAL SMILE

A smile is a magical gift;
It will love you to bits.

A smile is calm and safe,
Takes you to a peaceful place.

A smile is like
A hundred kind words,
Forever holding its worth.

A smile is romantic and true,
Warms your heart through-and-through.

A smile reaches for a mile
Offering us eternal style.

A smile is the essence of giving,
Makes life worth living.

A smile writes a beautiful poem
That takes our soul home.

THIS NEW EDEN

This land where I live, a man can walk free,
No matter what time of day.
There are so many places you don't wanna be,
But in NZ we all walk the same way.

In this world fights rage—one against another,
Can't people see reflections in others?
We may be of different race, religion or creed,
But when life goes wrong we have the same needs.

Where I live is in New Zealand,
Those who visit, love our land.
From high hills to hot water, we have lots to offer.
We are one nation—make New Zealand your plan.

You can ski in the Alps, or fish lakes for trout,
Or just take a trek in the bush,
NZ is the spot, yes, we've got the lot—Why stall—
Are you wanting a push?

There's no need to travel right round the whole world—
Experience it all in New Zealand.
Feel free to come here and give it a whirl,
In our country, my home: this new Eden.

GREAT APPRECIATION

Through the island of north,
Travelling down the line
Cruising along sun-baked
And (so it seemed) endless straights.

Enduring an 18-hour south-bound trip.
Driving by bus deep into
Browning, weather-scorched hills,
Unique in shape, pounded by
Forces of nature
Through millennia of ages.

Then winding down
Into gorges and gullies,
Twisting like a snake deep in
Damp valley dips.

The trickling streams rich from days of old,
Full of ancient gold,
When the pioneers with
Skimming pans in hand
Knee deep in the white water
Searched for the yellow rock.

Thinking of fortune and fame in their wake
Sieving for mountain gold
Around the clock
To win a claim at their stake.

These sites of awesome amazement
Start to take harbour in my mind,
Leaving me defenceless, compelled
To express these inner thoughts
At this point of time.

I feel privileged to be part of
Nature's beautiful world,
This sense of oneness and unity
My own hand in life's deal.

It's a major block in place
For inward growth,
One that Mother Nature's hands
Help to build.

Back to the trip:
Break stops at various townships
A chance to stretch the body,
Get out of that seat!

Break repetition of movement and out of the heat.
Nice pictures in view of glorious scenery.

A moment to mix and mingle with the locals
They offer passing chat
A friendly smile from their sun-soaked land—
Their chunk of paradise.
At our expense we give ourselves
In humble gesture and attitude alike.

Morning tea was delicious,
Lunch a delight.
One thing concerned me though:
Six dollars for the damn pie!

Terrific it was meeting the country-style folk
And the freedoms of farm life
Brings me back to earth.
These families are happy and content
Compared to inner-city life,
With all the fast-living drudgery
And hustle-bustle strife.

Once again another building block
Cemented in my quest for growth.
This one of course
Shows better judgment to those
Who may be in your sights to boast?
For we are all equal
Just live inland or on the coast.

Continuing down the island we go,
Then observing a subject worth debate,
I see paddock after paddock
Fence connecting fence
And countless farm gates,

The homes of many animals
Some of which to speak
Are pigs, cows and chickens, but most of all the sheep.
If only they knew their destiny.
If they only knew their fate . . .

Honest farmers making a living,
Breed quota to meet, demanding targets;
Stock wrapped and packed
Picked and shipped
To local markets.

The food chain in action;
A gruelling sight to see.
Our method not so grotesque, however,
As some of our planet's species.
Been going on since the dawn of time.
We all have to eat, that's a fact:
Part of human reality!

I guess it's survival of the fittest, a necessity,
A main part of existence:
Guilty as charged, you and me.
And, hey, who said that's not another
Building block of growth:
The Art of Savagery?
It's one we don't talk about but, hey . . .
Fresh meat: get stuck in, yummy !

The tour bus, crew and passengers,
Long past our destination south,
Now on the (home straight) of our return
With still a few miles to burn.
Been an interesting trip
Standing side by side,
Shaking hands with our
Native kiwi fern.

I have enjoyed the
Landscape of our awesome country,
With all its magnificence;
A wonderful journey of growth.
Much have I learned.

The building blocks of life
Are waiting for you, to discover
There are so many for the taking;
Just get out there, grab one
And search for another.

You see I believe we have a freedom called
"choice"
Lives deep within us all,
A constant ringing in our inner ear,
Tailored for us to hear:
A powerful voice.

The secret is:
Greatly appreciate the little things
That often pass our way and fall.
Catch them now,
Let them teach you,
But most importantly of all,

Build your growth blocks
Until your house is complete.
They will protect and guide your spirit,
Keep you happy and sweet.

Stay enlightened,
Shine your aura wide and tall,
Give great appreciation
Of everything and all.

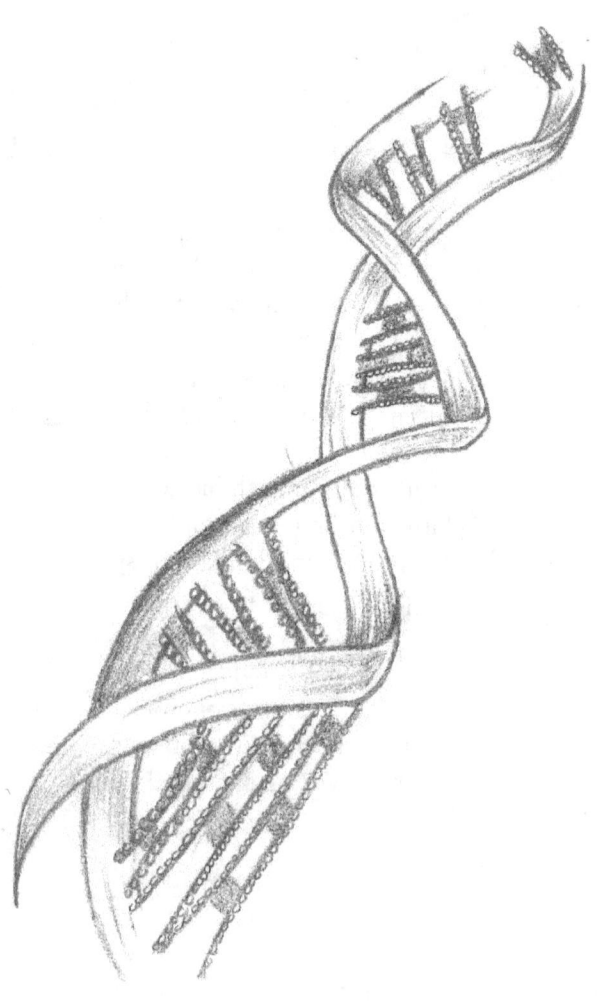

DNA SHOW

Why, oh why,
Do the Radiant eyes of the ancient sun
Insist on flirting
With flourishing fields
Since the birth of earth
Until each land has sprung?

And explain to me why
The Romantic moon's seasoned face
Begins to smile and glow
As it plays and shows off
Come dusk amongst the clouds
On to the vast blue ocean paths below.

You see in the beginning
There was the DNA show—
A story worth telling,
An amazing love affair.
DNA's courtship with sexy little cells
Within bounds of universal laws compelling.

Energetically creating and shaping
Molding and evolving with innocent cells
Both crafting and grafting, growing and changing
To nature's environment they understand so well.

As time passed and thanks to the show
Created was man
And with one spare rib in hand
Appeared woman,
Attracted by her natural beauty and developing curves
In love with her he was falling.

They discovered two appropriate gifts
Made to fit were wrap around fig tree leaves
Showcasing humans first designer briefs.

Man posed his new formed body
For her to dominate and take
Confident and keen
In his element of faith.

Surprised by testosterone exploding
Deep in manhood's core
Alas, unusual behaviour forthcoming
She just couldn't handle any more.

Of this mindful woman suggested to man,
This is a Garden . . . there are rules.
If you don't like it, buddy,
Sit and swivel on that—then let time pass
As she abruptly pointed
To a new sprouting bush
Called prickle grass!

But her need for man is strong
And fortunate he is to know.
Compassionately she allows him to stay
And help the relationship grow.

It's a great day
When a woman loves her man.
It's like the sun on heat
As it appears amorous
To nature's naked land.

Now in desperation
To perform the deed
In order to start the human family,
Very quietly they agree to
Tiptoe behind the apple tree.
Now the story is nearly complete.

Their love is like
The serenading moon's illuminating glow
Reflecting magical light
Upon the calm and mirrored ocean paths below,
And wow, it's just evolution at its best, you know.
In one of nature's most spectacular shows!

Now sharing life on earth equally,
A union of two humans very happy,
Man and Woman together,
Becoming one family forever.

So congratulations to DNA in the beginning
For courting sexy little cells.
End result:
Human race and civilisation
. . . Didn't DNA do well!

REASONABLE SENSE

Romantically tuned
Contests amicable stead
Caution to my desires
Only on lend.

Treading emotional ground
Versus reasonable sense
Be wary of ice thin
A broken heart's the end.

Loyalty harbours friendship
Commitment reflects respect
Developing trusting relationships
Will surely pass you on life's test.

THE NATURE OF LOVE

Whilst it is clear soul governs heart,
Heart has the ability to dictate from the start.
Strength of spirit wins soul the deal,
But heart leads with passion to claim and steal.

It is true
Sometimes heart wins on the day,
But soul is the boss
We do it my way.
Together they argue, fight and fuss;
Maybe it's time for them to discuss.

Both sit back, have their say and listen.
Heart talks within, no points missing;
Soul speaks wisely calling on power from above;
The subject, of course:
The nature of love.

She has a beautiful smile
It radiates within.
A keen sense of humour,
Friendly and loving.
Her beauty is surreal,
Nobody would protest
She must be an angel,
Or maybe a princess.

I say to you soul, declares heart with conviction,
I love her more than you care to listen.
She has a warm heart just like mine
Together beating until the end of time.

Huh if that's all you got,
Replied soul on a roll,
You see I met her first and you're just too old.
We walk hand in hand on life's bridge of dreams
Now and forever just her and me!

Heart and soul need to work together,
If indeed they are ever going to get her.
They simply adore her both alike
She is their darling
Their breath of life.

They decide to ask her:
Who is your true love?
Will it be heart from within?
Or soul from above?

Please tell us, demanded heart expressing emotion,
Make a decision, suggested soul with a notion.

Ok you boys, princess softly begins,
I love you both equally stop fighting and listen.
Heart, you are loyal, caring and true;
I certainly have strong feelings incredibly for you.
But without your soul's wisdom
Who's going to guide you?

And soul, oh, soul, what can I say?
Life without you could never be the same.
We may waltz and dance across fields of dreams
But without your heart's passion
Love would mean nothing.

With those words spoken so honest and smart,
Heart and soul decide a fresh start.
Ok, said heart, *soul you be the leader.*
I will devote all my love to her,
That's the way I'll treat her.

Soul's aura shines a sigh of relief.
Well, thank you, heart,
Now in you I believe.
Can you help me with this thing called love?
And in return I'll sail the three of us
To amazing horizons far above.

Princess seems happy they worked it out;
A tremendous job, without a doubt.

Herself, heart and soul,
Together as one,
Romantically riding
Natural wings of a dove.

Their dreams came true
A new journey begun:
It's a magical gift, you know.
It's quite simply
The nature of love.

HEART AND SOUL

Heart and soul—romantic duets,
Singing sweet love songs to their princess.
Soul surrendering his voice to her,
Serenading lyrics so clear and pure.
Joyful with hope for their love to endure,
Her beauty is amazing—of that, soul is sure.

Heart has much passion larger than life
Beating for her to keep love alive.
Capturing her eye his ambition and aim,
Without his princess he feels heartache and pain.
If it were true that heart could speak,
I love you my darling, would be words complete.

Heart and soul now understand each other,
Sharing their love helped them discover;
Work as a team and they will achieve
Undying love from their princess queen.

Heart has a question he asks of soul
Why does my heart beat out of control?
Whenever I'm near her it beats bold and fast
My passion for her must surely last.

Soul answers with a similar reply:
Heart, your predicament is the same as mine.
My soul glows brightly when she stands by me,
Strengthening my spirit incredibly.

But heart and soul are confused and unsure
Whether princess loves them for ever more.
So they pretend to argue, creating a tension,
In the cunning hope of gaining her attention.

What's wrong with you both? princess quietly asks.
I thought you were friends at long last.
Ok, can we talk today?
But one at a time,
You can each have your say.
Both speak your mind.

I love her more than you, heart and soul contest each other.
We may have the same blood but certainly ain't brothers!
Their little story getting a bit lame,
Didn't take princess long to figure out the game.

Oh dear heart, she says, *you're funny and cute,*
The way you get nervous when I am with you.
Express your passion well,
Stay honest and true.
Nothing to worry about:
I still love you.

My oh my, soul, it's nice talking to you.
I see through your game,
But your words are true.
Stay strong for me,
Because you must lead us:
Myself, heart and you to that place called love.

Descended from heavens a world apart
Where angels of beauty so graceful did start.
Radiant in aura, magnificently bright,
Delicate but daring, fearless in fight.

Heart and soul are lucky to have princess,
A dream come true, their very best.
With passion and strength by her side,
New horizons together they fly.

Radiant like an angel, heart and soul insist;
A wonder of beauty:
She is their Princess.

THE POWER OF SUGGESTION

If we ever consider the meaning of suggestion,
We should order our thoughts by way of selection.
Perfecting suggestion requires more reflection;
May it lead to conclusions well worthy of mention.

The beginning of thought is imagination—
Create and translate, formulate your vision;
Clarify intention, discuss your decision;
Stress with conviction, express your opinion.

Be inspiring, shift concepts around,
Identify content, confirm what you've found.
Arrange and structure, design with sound.
Edit wisely, be insightful as well as profound.

Apply mental imagery, develop the craft;
Visualization is the key; perfect the art.
Incorporate with action, just make a start—
The power of suggestion will set you apart.

Raise your aspirations within bounds to achieve;
Cause and effect will let you receive.
Colour your mind with a sense of being,
Your offering will be formed and utterly complete.

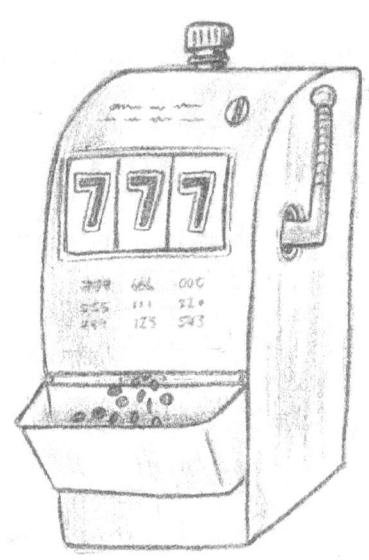

THE LONESOME GAMBLER

If there's One Thing I understand, I am a Gambling Man
To make some money—yeah! To win as much as I can.
You see, just the other day the hand of luck failed to go my way.
I lost miserably, the machine beat me again, just the other day.
I want it back, it belongs to me; I need to win it back—seriously.

So In my car I drive, I drive to the city in the sky.
I can win it back there, collect it all; it belongs to me, it's all mine.
Flashing lights blind my vision, yet here I am now in a
Spur-of-a-moment decision.
Should I be here, I quiz myself, is it right?
Do I care? Not in the least! It's going to be my night!

I need coin now as I reach into my pocket,
Shovel it into the machine, there it goes, damn, I need more.
As I instantly fling open my wallet.
Note after note, straight in they go.
Do I care? Not in the least, I don't want to know!
I just want my money back now—today, not tomorrow.

It's a full house in the city of sky tonight indeed.
Ethnic groups of all kinds, origins of many,
All having a good time tonight, so it seems.
Why am I so desperate to win, what's wrong with me?
My behaviour compulsive and impulsive—it's got to be pure greed!

I've been down this road before, it's all too familiar.
Why, oh, why am I walking down this highway of
The Lonesome Gambler?
Oh no! . . . I realize my money's getting low.
I gotta stop! I gotta stop!, but how can
I? I can't I can't, not until I win back my load.

Six hours pass, a long battle it's been.
I think I've been defeated again by that damn hungry money machine.
Then an alarming thought takes harbour in my mind:
I'm down a few grand now, my oh my!
Bugger . . . I say to myself. Just one more time, got to play my bet high;
Never know: might win the elusive three of a kind!

Finally I head for the door. It's all good, I kid myself,
I've been through this all before.
You see I couldn't accept the loss as Mr Denial took over.
Forget about it, he says. *I'm the Boss!*
You'll be right, mate—you'll win it all back tomorrow.

Question:
How to stop when you've lost?
Answer:
Put more in until you win!

The ravings of the Mad-man Rambler
What's his name?
Just call me. The Lonesome Gambler!

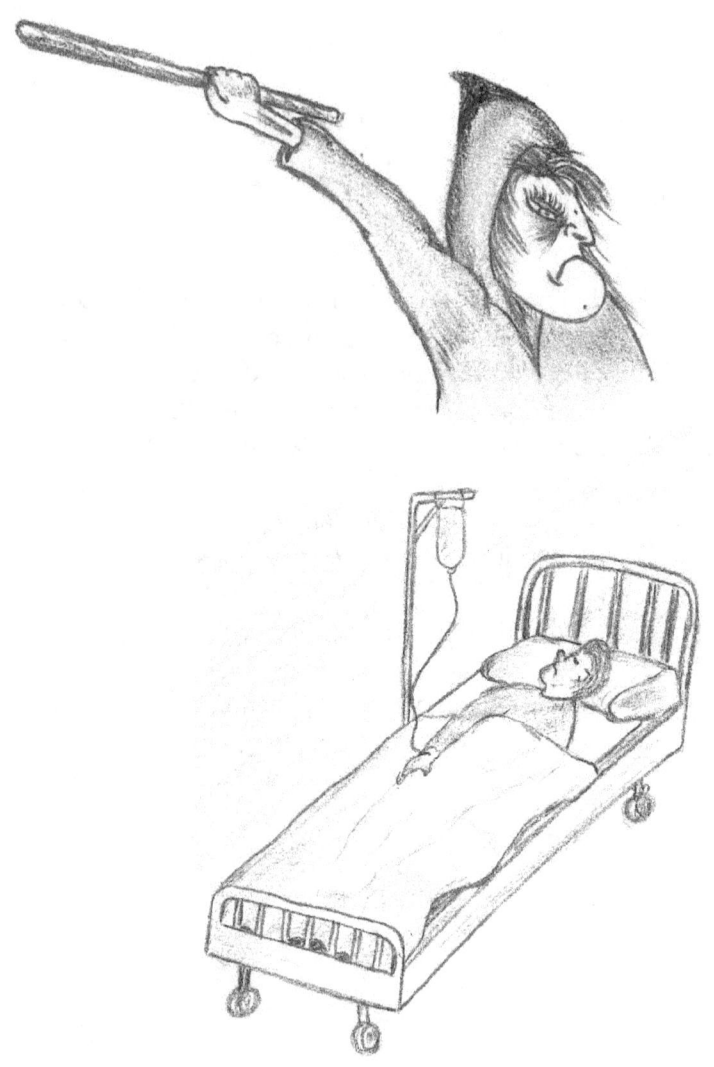

DESTINY OF PAIN

I awake each morning to be greeted by pain,
They say she's my friend but I know not her name.
Lying flat on my back, running riot through my veins,
She strikes with her hammer and whips with her cane.

We abide here together on floor 7 ward 73,
The land of waterworld called urology.
Auckland Hospital's the location and, hey, it's completely free!
But visit at your peril—with pain lurking, you may never leave.

The doctors, nurses, specialists and surgeons
Are all here to help us but sometimes confuse us.
They operate and say, you'll be fine, just believe us
But some hours go by and pain's back to tease us.

As time passes fast dawn grows to dusk,
Day follows day, may turn to a month.
The orderlies, medics and experts we trust
Show complete, honest commitment in caring for us.

They labour and serve around the clock;
Call it showing compassion 24 / 7 nonstop.
Congratulations to those medical teams; Healing's
their theme, recovery, their plot.

Now we come back to that one they call pain:
Remember that friend who inflicts riot with no name?
Time to put her on the stand, let Judgment fall today.
Let's steal her hammer and snap her cane!

But in her defence, pain loudly protested:
It's not my fault your body has been infected!
My sole purpose in life is to be your protector,
I'll find that intruder and alarm you when detected.

I'd also like to add, said pain on a roll,
Without me on the job, you have no control.
For your doctors, nurses, specialists and surgeons,
Not to mention your orderlies, medics and experts,
Would all labour hard to pinpoint the problem,
For without my assistance, the job is forgotten!

Hospital Hotel's not a bad place to be.
I mean we were born here, may die here-C'est la vie.
So cheers to those working in health care and needs,
Keep it rocking and rolling yeah! you should feel proud and pleased.

Now is to deem and decide pain's fate;
Has she been honest and true in defending her case?
Verdict reached ...
We say she keeps her mighty striking hammer and her kinky cane
Both go down in history her graceful claim to fame.

Now one question remains, the most important of all: For
our innocent friend pain, who stands now radiantly tall,
Deserves a great name, a tide after all how about:
Our **Guardian Protector.**
Pain's destiny fulfilled.

LIFE OF PAIN

Once again welcomed by pain,
Still swinging the hammer and holding high that cane
I realize the predicament facing me now:
This is beyond belief and I'm feeling down.

The orderly carries my bag, not uttering a sound.
Auckland Hospital ward 75; this time around,
There's an eerie feeling lurking in the air.
Drops my bag at bed's edge then disappears.

At Hospital Hotel to improve my health,
Pain waits patiently I feel it within self.
Hidden in shadows, prepares to pounce.
My anxiety multiplies into fear and doubt.

With surgery now over I wearily awake.
Surrounding medics deliver me faith,
Remanded secure, protection in place,
Methodically, pain tries to reclaim my fate.

Many days pass, all is going well.
That old foe pain is nowhere to be found.
Continued medication comforts me for now.
Confidence is growing as I'm healing very well.

Health has increased, my stay is at an end:
We are discharging you today, the kind registrar said.
Walk as pain permits, these crutches we'll lend
Strengthen with exercise until you mend.
Time passes
A surprise attack forced my body stiff.
Possession, I gasped as pain took firm grip.
Paralysed in statue with pain infiltrating,
To core of my bone, scraping and grating.

Poison running riot, flowing through my veins;
This must be her day, pain won again,
Striking with hammer
And whipping her cane.

The orderlies and nurses help me back to orthopaedics;
Another examination required is the thesis.
Please wait for the surgeon, the doctor insists;
Pain gives them proof my condition is worse.

Where are you now? the surgeon asks pain.
Show the location by using your cane.
Oh, so you now want my help? pain sarcastically quips.
So be it, pain says as she strikes and she whips.

I complain in agony and point to the spot;
The medical team moves in for the OP.
A complete success foiled pain's plot;
But, alas pain never dies, and never does it stop.

So onto the stand once again pain is called,
To explain why she inflicts terrible feeling to us all.
Pain's been giving us grief since early mankind,
Swinging hammer and cane from the dawn of time.

But in pain's defence, she makes explanation:
I'm selected to do this job for your information;
The nature of my work is to be cruel to be kind,
Using hammer and cane for the good of mankind.

I'd also like to add, pain firmly suggests,
Without my help your body is stressed.
Bacteria's ruthless gang often ruins your life
By launching my counter attack I whip and I strike;
Sometimes a tough battle, but I always win my fight!

Now with bag in hand outside Hospital Hotel I stand,
Body now healed, perfect to plan,
All medical teams to be commended and praised
As they work close with pain each and every day.

The re-trial concludes, the Jury returns;
Verdict reached—Justice served:
Not guilty, Your Honour! echoes in the court.
Pain is now innocent to continue her work.

One important detail left unfinished:
Pain's good name needs to be re-established.
We all live with pain in life until death,
It's my privilege to name pain our . . .
"Beginning and End."

LIFE

My name is Life, I am the beginning of all things.
I am the power of growth and evolution,
My purpose is to multiply species by reproduction,
Utilizing the environment to achieve this solution.

There are certain things I need to survive
The right atmosphere and adequate sunlight,
Water and nutrients the earth will provide
I leave the rest to my old friend Time.

It's my pleasure to be Life; please listen to me:
I offer you existence, a free opportunity.
You are the miracle of Life; I have created
A long time for you, the universe has waited.

When your journey on earth has had its day
I will travel with you through Death's doorway.
Fear not, dear friend, your soul you can bring.
My name is Life; I am the beginning of all things.

TIME

My name is Time; I am infinite by design,
Structuring the universe with systematic incline.
I navigate length using synchronization,
My mathematical formula is complex information.

I am the measure for the sequence of events
My workload endless, extremely immense.
Call me the pendulum that swings, the calendar of life;
I am accuracy itself, rhyming motion to time.

My main task of course is to follow this instruction:
Provide time for life to enjoy growth and reproduction.
I am the teacher of patience and perseverance;
Together, life and I give you quality existence.

Your journey with me is longer than you know—
After passing the next doorway, together we go,
Your life, your soul and I, for a never-ending ride.
For my name is Time and I am infinite—by design.

DEATH

My name is Death, I am as ancient as time.
I lurk deep in the oceans and watch from the sky,
I manage the seasons controlling day and night,
Ensuring all life cycles stay calibrated with time.

I hold your blueprints, the architect of your design,
Your biological functions (on my say) will resign,
I will contract disease on you if it's your time,
Or call my old friend Age to extend your life.

It's my honour to be Death, please let me explain:
My comrade, Life, and I play the same game,
For Death harbours Life and Life leads to Death.
It's the cycle of existence we should all comprehend.

I am the doorway that life passes through,
I'll chauffeur your soul-yes, I will guide you.
So fear me not, your Life will be fine,
My name is Death, I am as ancient as Time.

SOUL

My name is Soul, I live within all.
I occupy your body the moment you're born.
My purpose is to unite body and mind with me
    Teach you to grow and share love eternally.

I am invisible bur you see me in dreams.
I have no voice but you hear me subconsciously.
I don't have a pulse yet I dwell in your heart,
    My origins lie where imagination starts.

I live in harmony with Life, Death and Time.
Their plan for you is the same as mine:
Cherish your body well, it is the temple of my home
In return I give you immortality, never to be alone.

Look deep inside you'll need me one day,
Hand in hand we'll walk through death's doorway.
So let's have some fun before we get called.
My name is Soul and I live within all.

FAITH

Faith is to hear words unspoken
Faith is to feel actions not moving
Faith is to see imagination forming
Faith is to sense a great day dawning.

Faith is to know when things are uncertain
Faith is the 'show' behind closed curtains
Faith is to wait when time has run out
Faith is to call when there's no one about.

Faith is to talk when we have little to say
Faith is to smile when things don't go our way
Faith is to run when our legs are weak
Faith is to dream when we are asleep.

Faith is to challenge the impossible task
Faith is to compete for first not last
Faith is to embrace our journey through life
Faith is to trust that we will all survive.

THE OBVIOUS IS NOT ALWAYS RIGHT

Here I stand at life's grand entrance,
The surge of uncertainty flows through my being.
Not knowing my direction, stationary in stance,
I then follow the obvious, blindly believing.

Down life's swirling tunnel, tumbling I go.
Something's not right, I sense (of course).
Why am I here? I'd desperately like to know
As deeper into predicament's chaos I fall.

Finally the answer dawns on me gradually—
Following the obvious is not always right.
I must evaluate my options sensibly,
Show courage and integrity to win my fight.

So I dare to be different and follow my own star
Transforming my dreams into reality,
Achieving my goals, in a good role so far.
My true Destiny now lies before me.

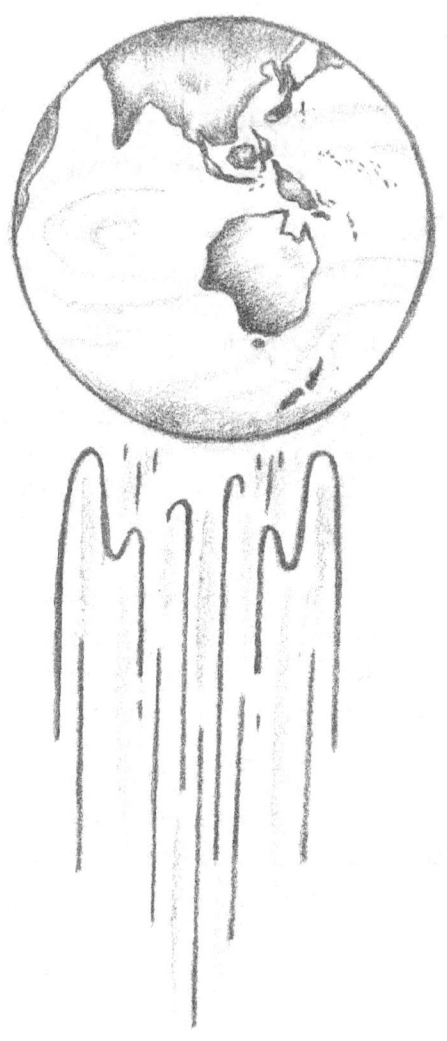

RISING TOGETHER

As we live through the seasons
There are so many reasons
We should think of to rise:
Create real life art,
It's an idea to start,
Paint it with friendship and memorize.

It won't happen in a day,
Show patience to gain
A little taste of your prize,
Consider what's at stake.
Find your spirit and take;
Go forth into the world with open eyes.

Looking back on our lives,
Reflecting on good times,
As we analyze each stage by day,
With confidence growing,
Shining and showing
In moments of our living wake.

Keeping peace with those
Friends and foes,
Learning by our mistakes,
But with personal demons yet to face
And old habits still to break;
Could it be time to evaluate?

With a need for recognition
To improve our position
Time to raise the bar.
Searching deep into self,
Taking heed of our wealth,
A show for the world to consider.

Competition a thought;
Practice be taught,
Rise and shine your star,
Time to have a shot
On a pitch and toss,
New exciting days we have come thus far.

Opportunities presenting,
Finally implementing.
A sense of pride to get ourselves sorted,
Compliments coming our way,
Self-respect here to stay;
Negative attitudes subsiding and thwarted.

A new stage of life fully awake and alive,
Those old demons gone, no longer taunted.
With energy flourishing,
Increasing not diminishing,
No more looking back,
Just up and forward.

Now keen and getting wise,
We have begun to rise
In order to present our best,
With insight and pride now on our side.
Team effort on the agenda:
Let it commence.

The privilege of excellence,
The comfort of confidence,
Both working together: true magnificence.
We are on our way, friends,
Find inner centre, focus and transcend,
Then we've passed our most difficult test.

Stand strong in who we are,
Know ourselves and follow each other
Side by side rise together,
Organize our life
To assist those in strife
And help out in stormy weather.

Live with compassionate will,
Use multitasking skill,
Be each other's staunch defender,
Strength in numbers
Beats the power of one.
Stay true to all and self forever.

This journey
In life
Will be so much better
If we
All spend it
Rising together.

MOTHER AND FATHER

The first thing we feel in life is mother's nurturing style.
The second thing we see is her beautiful smile.
We owe our life to mother for weaving our nest.
We love her dearly; our mother's the best.

The third, we remember, is a secure feeling of comfort
And the fourth is that, thanks to mum, now we've made it.
Walking, talking, having a grand time;
We owe our life to mother, so wonderful and kind.

The fifth was learning, so challenging and great.
The sixth, of course, practising family traits,
And, yeah, it was mum pointing out our mistakes!
She taught us to love—we learnt in her wake.

As we consider life, family and friends,
Mother is the one who really transcends.
She looks after us, she really does care,
Close to our hearts, mum, we keep you near.

And then there was dad who through his life showed
That hard work was easy—we reap what we sow.
You're a patient man, that we know;
In tune with nature, you would walk
Across scorching deserts, through rain and snow.

You're not a big talker you don't like to boast
Loyalty and integrity are the strengths we like the most.
You created a family, raised them well,
Put us back on our feet at times when we fell.

You're an awesome man: our dad, our host.
Congratulations mum and dad—
We love you both the most.

FOREVERMORE

Forevermore, long may you live forevermore.
A voice will call you to heaven's door,
Shining white lights will guide you there,
Great golden harps playing for your ears
Forevermore—long may you all live forevermore.
In life you showed us all the way:
To live in the present and keep the faith.
Always stand tall—rise if you fall—
Keep your head high and reach for the sky.
Your colourful soul be remembered by all.
Long may you live forevermore.
Nature's wings will fly you for the ride
Into your lifetime's great other side.
They will greet you so happily,
The Saints, Angels and Family,
And there's no better place a soul could be,
Than in heaven's great palace of serenity:
Playing on cloud's comfortable swings,
Resting on floating, age-old leaves,
Thrilling the spirit on destiny's breeze;
Laughs and warm smiles so contentedly;
The time has now come for your walk in awe
To that golden pathway onto heaven's dance floor.
So waltz on in and we'll see you for sure.
Together as one,
Forevermore.

www.ingramcontent.com/pod-product-compliance
Lightning Source LLC
LaVergne TN
LVHW012059070526
838200LV00070BA/3256